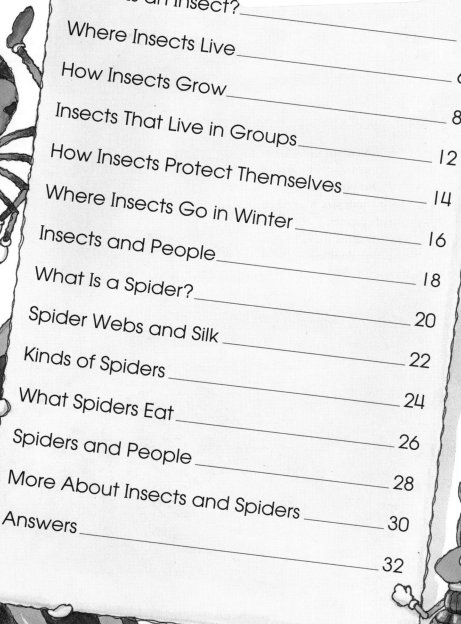

Inse...

What Is an Insect?

Like you, insects are alive. Both people and insects are animals. But insects don't have bones inside their bodies as you do. Instead, they have a hard outside shell. Insects are different from other animals because they have six legs. Most adult insects have wings.

An insect's body has three main parts.

The **abdomen** is the "tail" end of the insect. Inside are the heart and breathing tubes. Some insects, such as bees, have a stinger on the end of the abdomen.

The **head** has eyes, antennae (an-**ten**-ee), and the parts that eat.

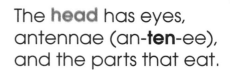

Write Now!

Yikes! Some kid just put you in a jar for an hour. What was it like? Take out a sheet of paper and write.

The **thorax** is right behind the head. The wings and legs are connected to the thorax.

Ladybug, ladybird, lady beetle—whatever you call me, I'm an insect.

What's That Part?

Write the name of the part under each insect.

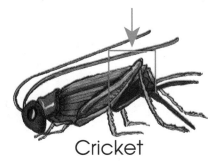

Cricket

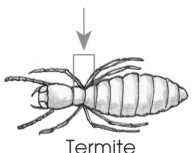

Termite

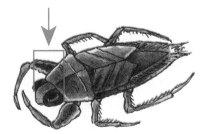

Giant waterbug

Invent an Insect

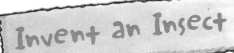

Imagine that you discover a new kind of insect. Draw your discovery. Make sure your insect has three main body parts, six legs, and two antennae.

Make a Bug Catcher

To make a bug catcher, ask an adult to cut the top from a clear plastic bottle. Make a screen by cutting a slit in a piece of fabric. Attach it over the opening with a rubber band. Then go on a bug hunt. When you find an interesting bug, put it in the bottle.

Take your bug catcher into the shade. Look at the bug carefully. Is it an insect? Write notes or draw pictures. Keep the bug no longer than an hour. Bugs need to find their own food, water, and shelter.

Insect Count

Not all crawlers and wrigglers are insects. Some tiny creatures have a hard covering and legs with joints, but the wrong number of legs. Some have soft, slimy bodies.

Take a close look at each animal. Count the legs. Then write its name under **Insects** or **Not Insects**.

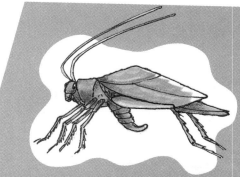

Katydid
Some people say the noise katydids make at night sounds like their name.

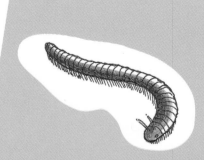

Millipede
Some millipedes give off a big stink if they are frightened.

Pill bug
Pill bugs roll up in a tight ball when disturbed. Can you guess how they got their name?

Slug
Slugs leave a slimy trail when they move about.

Butterfly
The spots on the wings of this butterfly look like eyes and confuse the butterfly's enemies.

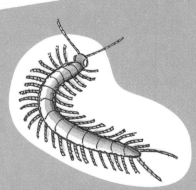

Centipede
Centipedes live under rotting logs and in other damp places.

Earthworm
Earthworms dig burrows in soil. They come out at night.

Dog tick
Ticks suck the blood of dogs, cows, horses, and humans.

Tarantula
Some people think these fuzzy creatures make gentle pets.

Dragonfly
Dragonflies catch mosquitoes and eat them.

Insects	Not Insects

What do you call a rabbit owned by a beetle?

A bug's bunny.

Awesome!

Insects don't have voices. But many insects make noises by rubbing parts of their body together. Have you heard a cricket's song? The cricket rubs its front wings together to make a cheerful sound.

Where Insects Live

Insects live on dry land just about everywhere. In really cold places, such as the North Pole, they live in the fur of polar bears and other big, warm animals. In hot places, rain forests for example, insects are everywhere you look.

A few kinds of insects, but not too many, live in oceans. Quite a few kinds live in streams and ponds.

Watery Homes

Some kinds of insects live on or in water. Here are four of them.

Strider

Water boatman

Dragonfly nymph

Mayfly nymph

Look at the underwater scene. Circle a water strider red and a water boatman green. Draw a blue circle around a dragonfly nymph and a brown circle around a mayfly nymph. Then count each kind of water insect. Write the number of each kind.

Striders: _____   Water boatmen: _____   Dragonfly nymphs: _____   Mayfly nymphs: _____

Insects All Around Us

The picture shows lots of insects in places where they often live. Do you recognize any of these insects? Make a list of the ones you know.

Awesome!
Don't look for a cricket's ears on its head. Its ears are on its legs!

Insects I Know
_____
_____
_____
_____
_____
_____
_____
_____

monarch

walking stick

grasshopper

praying mantis

ant

bee

ladybug

Roll logs and rocks back where you find them. Then insects' homes are not destroyed.

How Insects Grow

Their hard outer skin helps insects. It's waterproof like a raincoat and protects like armor. The only problem is that insects' skin can't stretch. So, how do baby insects get bigger?

Insects get bigger when they climb out of the outside layer of their skin. After they slowly step out, the inner layer of their skin is soft and wet. It takes a while to dry and harden. While the insects wait, they can't run or fly away from enemies.

A Chinch Bug Grows Up

Have you ever seen this insect? It's a chinch bug. A young chinch bug looks like a small adult, except it has no wings.

Look at these pictures of a chinch bug. The youngest chinch bug is an egg. Each time the baby chinch bug shed its skin, it grew a little. Look at the ruler under each chinch bug. Number the chinch bugs in order from youngest to oldest. Write the numbers **1** through **5** under the correct pictures.

Every time an insect crawls out of its skin, it is growing up. Insects can't talk, but it's fun to pretend they can. Fill in the balloons to tell what they might say.

COOL WORD

An insect's hard skin is its **exoskeleton** (*eks*-oh-**skel**-uht-uhn).

All insects start life as tiny eggs. The babies of some insects look totally different from their mothers and fathers. After some amazing changes, the babies grow up to look just like their parents.

Egg
A monarch butterfly lays an egg on a plant. The egg looks like a jewel.

The Four Stages of a Monarch Butterfly's Life Cycle

Larva
Out of the egg walks a caterpillar, also called a larva. The monarch larva's job is to eat. As it eats, the larva outgrows and sheds its skin. This happens four or five times. Each time the larva gets a little bigger.

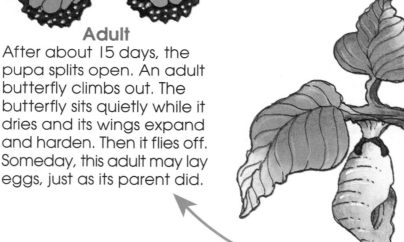

Adult
After about 15 days, the pupa splits open. An adult butterfly climbs out. The butterfly sits quietly while it dries and its wings expand and harden. Then it flies off. Someday, this adult may lay eggs, just as its parent did.

Pupa
After the larva reaches its full size, it is ready to become a pupa. The pupa hangs upside down from a twig or leaf, and its covering hardens. Inside the covering, butterfly parts are growing.

Monarch Word Search

Fill in the blanks with the words from the box. Then look for the words in the puzzle. Circle the words.

B	P	I	H	W	N	R	B	E	T	M
C	A	T	E	R	P	I	L	L	A	R
D	A	W	T	R	B	V	S	M	B	O
F	O	U	R	L	N	F	L	R	Q	R
O	T	B	U	T	T	E	R	F	L	Y
S	F	E	M	B	X	O	Y	R	M	A
K	S	T	R	L	V	S	L	N	E	Q
I	N	W	B	A	E	E	S	Y	C	P
N	P	S	D	R	I	G	T	O	K	U
I	L	R	T	V	E	G	G	J	Y	P
G	W	P	L	A	N	T	M	P	T	A

butterfly
four
larva
plant
caterpillar
pupa
egg
skin

1. An insect begins its life as an _____ .

2. The monarch butterfly lays its egg on a _____ .

3. The _____ comes out of the egg.

4. The larva is also called a _____ .

5. The monarch sheds its _____ during the larva stage.

6. During the pupa stage, a _____ is forming.

7. The butterfly comes out of the _____ .

8. The life cycle of a butterfly has _____ stages.

Insects That Live in Groups

Some kinds of insects live alone. Others live in big groups. Ants, bees, and wasps live in groups. An ant group is called a **colony**. The adult ants in the colony have different jobs. They work together to keep the colony alive.

Most ants dig an underground nest. It has tunnels and rooms. Some rooms are for the young larvae. Other rooms are for the pupa stage. Workers have sleeping rooms.

Why do bees hum? They forgot the words!

Queen
The queen lays eggs.

Food-getting worker
Some workers leave the nest to find food to bring home.

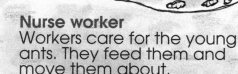

Nurse worker
Workers care for the young ants. They feed them and move them about.

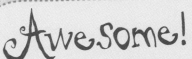

Awesome!

An ant can lift things that weigh 50 times more than it does. If you were as strong for your size as an ant is for its size, you could lift a car!

Special males and females
These males and females will leave the colony to mate and start new colonies of their own.

Have an Ant Picnic

One way to watch ants is to have a picnic. In this picnic, the treats are for the ants. For which foods do you think ants will come running?

You will need small samples of foods. Foods you might choose include fruit, cereal, cooked meat, cookies, honey, crackers, and lettuce.

1. List the foods you picked for your ant picnic in the chart below. Predict the food or foods the ants will choose first.

   _____

2. Put a small piece of each food on its own paper plate.

3. Find a little hill of dirt that shows where an ant colony is. Put the plates in a circle around the anthill.

4. Wait and watch. On the chart, write an **X** in the **1** column for the food the ants find first. Write an **X** in the **2** column for the food the ants eat second. Do the same for the rest of the food.

Was your prediction correct? _____

Foods	1	2	3	4	5

Write Now!

○ Be an ant or a bee with a BIG problem! You want to live all by yourself, not in a colony or hive.

○ What will you do? Take out a sheet of paper and write.

How Insects Protect Themselves

Bats eat insects. So do frogs, foxes, and birds. Many insects eat other kinds of insects. How do insects stay alive when so many creatures want to eat them?

Some insects taste bad. A bird may try to eat a monarch butterfly once. But the monarch tastes so terrible it will never try to eat one again!

Some insects protect themselves by stinging and biting. Wasps can give a painful sting. Insects that taste bad or sting have bright colors and patterns. This warns other animals to stay away, or else!

Keep away! I taste horrible!

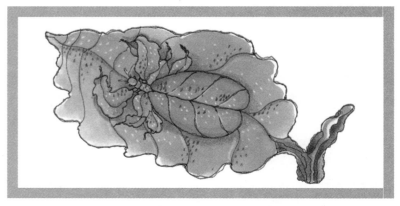

COOL WORD

Colors or shapes that hide an animal are **camouflage** (**kam**-uh-flazh).

Hiding keeps other insects safe. Their small size helps them hide. Having colors and shapes that blend with their hiding places helps, too.

Hide-and-Seek!

A walking stick that isn't walking is hard to find. This insect's shape and color make it look just like the twigs on which it sits. Find the walking sticks. Circle each one. How many can you find?

Number of walking sticks: _____

Make a Showoff Butterfly

Make a butterfly with warning colors on its wings.

1. Fold a piece of paper in half. Then draw a butterfly's body on the fold.

2. Put drops of paint on one side of the fold in the shape of two wings. Make a colorful design inside the wing on that side, too.

3. Press the two sides together. Open slowly to see two wings with warning colors.

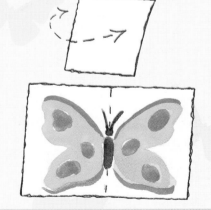

How Insects Protect Themselves

Where Insects Go in Winter

You can find insects in winter if you look carefully. Black dots moving on snow on a warm winter day are insects called snow fleas.

Most adult female insects die before winter comes. Before she dies, a praying mantis may make 15 egg cases. She makes a foam nest on a plant stem. Then she lays her eggs inside the foam. The foam dries and hardens. In spring, the eggs hatch and the babies climb out.

Awesome!

Millions of kinds of insects live in rain forests. Some of them, such as this giant weevil, look very strange to us.

Which Way Do I Go?

Some insects **migrate**, traveling to places with warm weather. Monarch butterflies are the world's most amazing insect travelers. Some monarchs that live in western North America spend the winter in sunny California. Monarchs in eastern North America fly south to warmer weather in Mexico.

If you live in the United States (except Hawaii and Alaska), find your state on this map. If it is a pink state, your monarchs may fly to California this fall. If you live in a green state, your monarchs will fly to Mexico for the winter. Draw a line to connect your butterflies' summer homes and winter homes.

Awesome!
If the burying beetle finds a dead mouse, the beetle buries it in the soil. Then the beetle lays its eggs nearby. When the eggs hatch, the baby beetles eat the mouse.

I fly up into the mountains for the winter. There I join hundreds of other ladybugs in a cave.

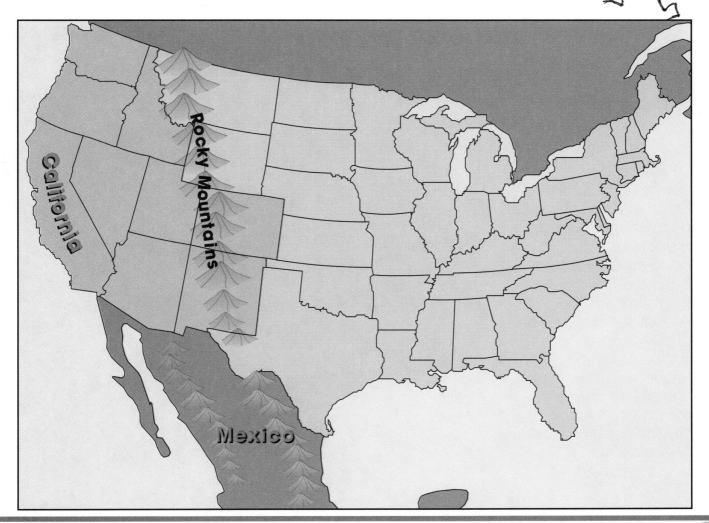

Insects and People

Do insects bug you? Mosquito bites itch. Ants and cockroaches get into food. Fleas bite our pets and sometimes ourselves. Other insects eat farmers' crops as the fruits and vegetables grow.

Insects do plenty of good things, though. Many plants can't live without insects. Without bees, we'd have no apples or honey to eat. Insects are food for birds and other animals. Ants and beetles help get rid of dead plants and animals on the ground.

What bug likes picnics, wears a red suit, and has a long white beard?

Ant-a-Claus!

Insect Count

How many insects can you find in this picture? _____

Awesome!

People around the world eat insects. In Arab countries, people munch locusts. Grasshoppers and waterbugs are considered treats in Asia. In South Africa, some people roast termites to eat like popcorn. In Mexico, bakers make a cake from water boatman eggs. Chocolate-covered ants might be served at parties in North America.

What's That Insect?

Fill in the blanks with words from the box. Then write the letters in the squares to find out which insect pest loves to munch wood.

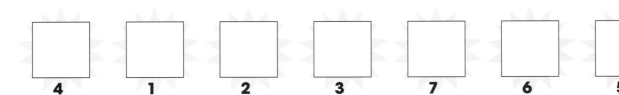

germs	soil
vegetables	honey
hatch	ants

1. Insects help fruit and __ __ __ __ __ __ __ __ __ grow.
   1

2. Some insects spread __ __ __ __ __ that make us ill.
   2 **3**

3. When insect eggs __ __ __ __ __ , the babies climb out.
   4

4. We like to eat __ __ __ __ __ made by bees.
   5

5. Tiny __ __ __ __ can spoil a picnic.
   6

6. Insects make the ground, or __ __ __ __ , healthy.
   7

4	**1**	**2**	**3**	**7**	**6**	**5**

What Is a Spider?

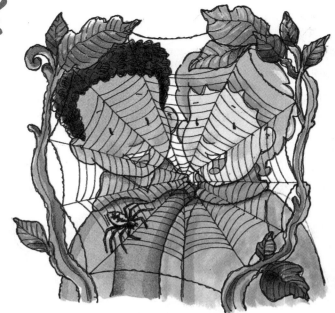

Like insects, spiders have a hard outside skin instead of bones. Spiders are different from insects in some ways. They have eight walking legs, not six. Spiders have two main body parts, not three. Spiders don't have wings or antennae.

Spiders have parts that look like short legs.

The legs are connected to the front of the body.

Most spiders have eight eyes.

The abdomen is the back part of the body.

Spiders have fangs with poison.

Spiders can spin silk with their spinnerets.

The prosoma is the front part of the spider's body.

Spider Eyes

Most spiders have eight eyes, but some have six, four, or two. Even with all those eyes, though, spiders can't see very well. They rely on their senses of smell and touch. Many spiders feel things through the hairs that cover their bodies.

Look at the spider faces. How many eyes do you see? On the last spider, draw two, four, six, or eight eyes.

Which Spider Is Different?

The spiders in each row are the same, right? Wrong! Circle the spider that is different from the first one in each row.

Crab spider

Common house spider

Black widow spider

Black-and-yellow garden spider

Spider Webs and Silk

All spiders make silk in their bodies. The silk comes out of the tail end of the abdomen.

Some spiders use these thin but strong threads to make webs. Webs trap insects and other small animals for the spider to eat.

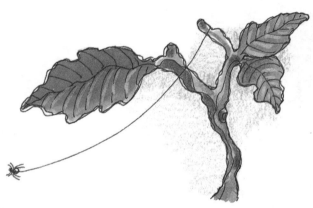

Some baby spiders use their own silk to leave the egg. The baby climbs to a high place. Then it lets out a line of silk into the wind. The wind pulls the silk and the spider is carried off. This way of traveling is called **ballooning**.

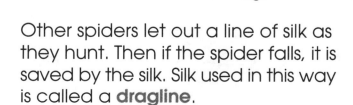

Most spiders wrap their eggs in silk. The silk makes a tight, soft bag called an **egg sac**.

Other spiders let out a line of silk as they hunt. Then if the spider falls, it is saved by the silk. Silk used in this way is called a **dragline**.

Spiderweb Puzzle

Use the clues to fill in the puzzle.

ACROSS

1. A spider's _____ make silk.

5. A spider's fangs hold _____ .

6. You may find _____ in a web.

DOWN

2. Webs are made of _____ .

3. A spider has _____ legs.

4. A spider's body has _____ parts.

silk	poison
insects	eight
spinnerets	two

Web Detective

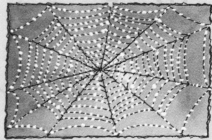

In the early morning, spider webs have tiny drops of dew, or water, on them. The drops sparkle in the sun and make the webs easy to see. You can make some "dew" with a spray bottle filled with water.

Take a walk with an adult in a park or a grassy field. Take a spray bottle, a notebook, and a pencil. Look for webs between the stems of tall flowers and grasses. Look between rocks and the ground, too. When you find a web, spray it gently with water. Draw or write what you see.

Kinds of Spiders

One way to group spiders is by how they catch their food. Web-spinning spiders wait for flying insects to get stuck in their webs. Hunting spiders chase insects or hide and wait for them to go by. Here are some examples of both kinds.

Why is a spider the best ballplayer? It's good at catching flies!

Web-spinning spiders

These spiders are easy to find. They make fancy webs that look like wagon wheels. These kinds of webs are **orb webs**. The garden spider's orb web can be over two feet around. Insects get trapped in the sticky web.

Cobweb spiders

Did you ever look up at the ceiling and see dust-covered threads hanging down? Those are the tangled silk webs of cobweb spiders. The cobwebs catch dust. They catch flies, too.

Hunting spiders

These spiders are hard to find. They slowly change color from white to yellow to match the flowers in which they hide. When a bee comes along, this crab spider grabs it.

Jumping spiders

A jumping spider walks slowly and then runs and jumps to catch its food.

Break the Spider Code!

Use the code to figure out the spider's message.

A=2	B=4	C=6	D=8	E=10	F=12
G=14	H=16	I=18	J=20	K=22	L=24	M=26
N=28	O=30	P=32	Q=34	R=36	S=38	T=40
U=42	V=44	W=46	X=48	Y=50	Z=52

16 10 24 32!

38 28 2 22 10 38,   12 36 30 14 38,

2 28 8   4 18 36 8 38   2 36 10   2 12 40 10 36

26 10!   40 16 10 50   46 2 28 40   40 30   10 2 40

26 10   12 30 36   24 42 28 6 16!

38 32 18 8 10 36

_____

_____

_____

_____

_____

What Spiders Eat

All spiders catch, kill, and eat other animals—most often insects. The spider sticks its fangs into an insect, and poison shoots into the insect and kills it.

Spiders cannot swallow chunks of food. So the spider puts liquids from its stomach into the body of the insect. The soft parts of the insect change to liquid. Then the spider slurps up the liquid food. The insect's hard outer skin is left over.

A few spiders eat other animals as well as insects. Some spiders eat other spiders. Tarantulas, which can be as big as your hand, may even catch small birds, mice, and lizards.

What did the spider say when she got a stomachache?

It must have been someone I ate!

What's for Lunch?

Suppose you have a restaurant just for spiders. What do you serve? Fill in the menu with delicious spider treats. Remember—spiders can only slurp, not chew.

Menu

Soups

Main Courses

Desserts

Drinks

What Spiders Eat

Spiders and People

Spiders are shy animals. They try to hide from people.

Spiders do people a favor by eating lots of insects that bug us. So don't bother spiders! Let them do their jobs.

People use spiders' silk in some surprising ways. Long ago, people used the strong silk to make fishing nets and traps to catch birds. Cobwebs were used as bandages. Today, very thin spider silk is used to make crosshairs in microscopes.

Think of something else for which strong, thin spider silk might be used. Write your suggestion on the line.

_____

A World of Insects and Spiders

Look at all the insects and spiders! Which ones do you remember seeing on other pages of this book? Color the picture. In the blank space, draw an insect or spider of your own.

Spiders and People

More About Insects and Spiders

Information Books

Amazing Insects by Laurence Mound

Amazing Spiders by Alexander Parson

The Big Bug Book by Margery Facklam

Bugs: A closer look at the world's tiny creatures by Jinny Johnson

Life of the Ladybug by Heiderose Fischer-Nagel and Andreas Fischer-Nagel

The Magic School Bus Inside a Beehive by Joanna Cole

Monster Bugs by Lucille Recht Penner

Spider Watching by Vivian French

Who Eats What? Food Chains and Food Webs by Patricia Lauber

Magazines

Chickadee

Owl

Ranger Rick

Your Big Backyard

Storybooks and Poetry

Animal, Vegetable, Mineral: Poems About Small Things by Myra Cohn Livingston

Antics! by Cathi Hepworth

Charlotte's Web by E.B. White

The Grouchy Ladybug by Eric Carle

The Very Busy Spider by Eric Carle

The Very Hungry Caterpillar by Eric Carle

Why Mosquitoes Buzz in People's Ears by Verna Ardema

Tapes

Insect. VHS. BBC Wildvisions

Butterflies. A videotape from Polygram

Charlotte's Web. VHS. Paramount

I'd Like to Be an Entomologist: Learning About Insects, Spiders and Other Arthropods. Audiotape and book. Twin Sisters Productions

Toys and Games

Backyard Bugs. A five-foot-long floor puzzle. A Frank Schaffer Publication

Butterfly Garden: Raise Painted Lady Butterflies–Then Release Them. Insect Lore USA

Explore the World of Insects. Terrarium from the Smithsonian Institution

What Animal Is That? Quiz Jigsaw Puzzle. Binary Arts

Computer Software

Eyewitness Encyclopedia of Nature

One Small Square: Backyard

SimAnt: The Electronic Ant Colony

How Many Bugs in a Box? CD-ROM

The Multimedia Bug Book. CD-ROM

Answers

Page 3
abdomen, thorax, head

Page 5

Insects	Not Insects
Katydid	Millipede
Butterfly	Pill bug
Dragonfly	Slug
	Centipede
	Earthworm
	Dog tick
	Tarantula

Page 11
1. egg	5. skin
2. plant	6. butterfly
3. larva	7. pupa
4. caterpillar	8. four

B	P	I	H	W	N	R	B	E	T	M
C	A	T	E	R	P	I	L	L	A	R
D	A	W	T	R	B	V	S	M	B	O
F	O	U	R	L	N	F	L	R	Q	R
O	T	B	U	T	T	E	R	F	L	Y
S	F	E	M	B	X	O	Y	R	M	A
K	S	T	R	L	V	S	L	N	E	Q
I	N	W	B	A	E	E	S	Y	C	P
N	P	S	D	R	I	G	T	O	K	U
I	L	R	T	V	E	G	G	J	Y	P
G	W	P	L	A	N	T	M	P	T	A

Page 19
1. vegetables
2. germs
3. hatch
4. honey
5. ants
6. soil

t e r m i t e

Page 6
Striders: 5
Water boatmen: 6
Dragonfly nymphs: 3
Mayfly nymphs: 4

Page 7
All the insects listed in the word box are shown in the picture.

Page 15

11 walking sticks

Page 21

Page 8

Page 18
total number of insects: 50
(includes fleas on and near dog)

Page 23

ACROSS	DOWN
1. spinnerets	2. silk
5. poison	3. eight
6. insects	4. two

```
      ²s
¹s p i n n ³e r e ⁴t s
  i       i       w
  l       g   ⁵p o i s o n
  k       h
⁶i n s e c t s
```

Page 25
HELP!
SNAKES, FROGS,
AND BIRDS ARE AFTER
ME! THEY WANT TO EAT
ME FOR LUNCH!
SPIDER

Page 27
Answers will vary, but all foods must be liquids.

REPTILES & AMPHIBIANS CONTENTS

WHAT IS A REPTILE?

How is a box turtle like a python? A crocodile like an iguana? A chameleon (kuh-**mee**-lee-uhn) like a lizard? All these animals are alike in one important way—they are reptiles.

My name's Camilla, and I'm a chameleon. Chameleons can change color. Meet some of my friends.

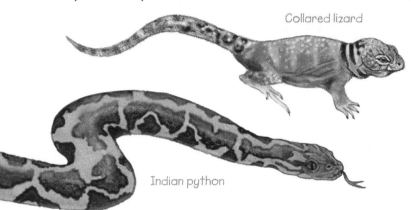

Collared lizard

Indian python

Nile crocodile

You can see that reptiles vary greatly in size, shape, and color. Like many animals, including humans, reptiles are vertebrates—animals with backbones. And like people, they use lungs to breathe.

Eastern box turtle

How Many Reptiles?

In this desert scene, all the animals are reptiles—except one. Circle the reptiles. Write the total number in the box.

number of reptiles _____
Which animal is *NOT* a reptile? Look carefully! _____

Look Inside!

Look at the crocodile's backbone and lungs. Then find those parts on the garter snake. Write lungs and backbone on the lines.

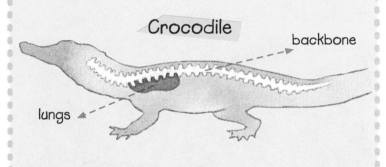

Crocodile

backbone

lungs

Reptile skin is dry and rough. The skin of lizards and snakes is made of overlapping scales. The scales of turtles and crocodiles grow into hard, bony plates.

Many kinds of reptiles shed their skin, or molt, several times a year. New scales grow under the old ones, and the skin loosens and falls off. Snakes crawl out of their old skin and leave it behind in one piece. Lizard skin comes off in big strips.

Their skin keeps water in reptiles' bodies for a long time. That's why so many kinds of reptiles can live in deserts and other dry places.

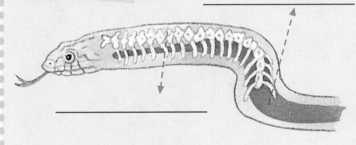

Garter Snake

_____

_____

Reptiles are cold-blooded animals. That means they have no built-in way to control the temperature of their bodies. When their surroundings are cold, they are cold. When it's warm out, they are warm. To stay alive, cold-blooded animals must not become extremely hot or cold. That's why you might see a snake sunning itself on a rock on a cool day. But if the day turns hot, the snake will find a shady place to cool off.

Reptiles live almost everywhere in the world, usually on land. Here are two places you will find reptiles.

Marshland

Jungle

Reptile Code

Put a letter in place of each number to finish the sentence. Then answer the question.

c	t	a	t	r	i	n	A
1	2	3	4	5	6	7	8

Snakes can be found on all continents except

☐ ☐ ☐ ☐ ☐ ☐ ☐ ☐ ☐ ☐
8   7   4   3   5   1   4   6   1   3

Can you guess why?

Most reptiles can see well. The kinds of reptiles that are active at night have long, narrow pupils, which can open very wide to let in as much light as possible. Reptiles that stay active during the day and sleep at night have round pupils.

Many reptiles can hear low sounds. Snakes can't hear sounds, though. They "hear" by feeling vibrations that travel through the ground. Most reptiles eat other animals. Some lizards and turtles eat mainly plants. Reptiles can go without food for a long time.

Stay Safe, Snake!

Help the snake get away from its enemies.

Reptile Review

Complete the sentences with the words below. Then write the words in the puzzle.

lungs   temperature

land   reptiles

backbone   plates

My tongue is really long. It's coated with sticky stuff that helps me catch prey.

AWESOME!
There are more than 6,000 kinds of reptiles. Some are as tiny as two inches long. Others are longer than 30 feet.

Across

2. Reptiles breathe air through _____.

5. Cold-blooded animals do not have a constant body _____.

6. Most reptiles live on _____.

Down

1. Reptile skin is made of scales or bony _____.

3. An animal that is a vertebrate has a _____.

4. Turtles, snakes, lizards, and crocodiles are all _____.

LEAPIN' LIZARDS

Green iguana

The earliest lizards lived on Earth about 200 million years ago during the time of the dinosaurs, their reptile cousins. Lizards come in many colors and sizes. Most walk on four legs, but some don't have any legs at all.

Chilean cave lizard

Five-lined skink

Lizards defend themselves in unusual ways. Some have tails that break off when they are attacked. The tail wriggles around and distracts the attacker while the lizard escapes. Luckily, the tail grows back. Some lizards bluff. They puff up their bodies and hiss while lashing their tails. Some lizards change colors for protection.

Cracks in the lizard's backbone mark weak places where the tail can break apart.

Lizard Code

Put a letter in place of each number to finish the sentence.

r	t	o	i	G	m	l	a	e	n	s
1	2	3	4	5	6	7	8	9	10	11

The only poisonous lizard in the United States is the

5	4	7	8		6	3	10	11	2	9	1
.

COOL WORD

Dinosaur means "terrible lizard." Unlike lizards, though, many dinosaurs walked on strong back legs.

Most lizards eat insects, slugs (snails without shells), and other small animals. The chameleon uses its long, sticky tongue to catch insects quicker than you can say *flick*!

Big lizards, such as Komodo dragons, eat pigs, deer, and other large animals. Some lizards, iguanas for example, are plant eaters.

Puzzling Lizards

Complete the sentences with the words below. Then write the words in the puzzle.

slugs
iguana
dinosaurs
tails
tongue
four

Across

1. Lizards lived during the time of the _____.

4. Most lizards walk on _____ legs.

5. A chameleon catches bugs with its long, sticky _____.

Down

2. One lizard that eats plants is the _____.

3. Some lizards eat_____.

5. Some lizards drop their_____ when they're in trouble.

Lizards really get around! Some swim and some fly—well, almost. A group of lizards called flying dragons glides from tree to tree the same way flying squirrels do.

Draco lizard

Most lizards scamper about using their sharp claws to hold on to rough surfaces. One kind, the gecko, has slits on its toes that act like suction cups to help it stick to things. Geckos can walk upside down on a ceiling or a pane of glass!

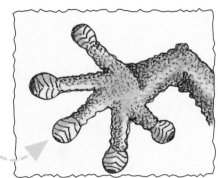

Some lizards that live on the ground, such as skinks, have very weak legs—or no legs at all.

AWESOME!

How do you tell a legless lizard from a snake? Lizards have eyelids and ear openings. Snakes don't have either one.

Great plains skink

Guess the Lizard

Use the clues to write the names of the lizards.

flying dragon   iguana   gecko   skink   Komodo dragon

1. I'm a real heavyweight. _____

2. Maybe I look like one, but I'm no snake. _____

3. My toes are the stickiest. _____

4. Let's eat a salad. _____

5. I glide through the air with the greatest of ease. _____

SLITHERING SNAKES

W hat's the biggest difference between snakes and most other reptiles? Right! Snakes have no legs. Most slide along the ground by squeezing the muscles attached to their backbones so that their bodies make loops. The loops push on the ground or in the water, and the snakes move forward. Snakes can twist their long, thin bodies every which way, even into tight balls, to protect themselves from enemies.

Indian cobra

Corn snake

Ribbon snake

Word Find

Circle four places where snakes can be found. Look ↑, ↗ and ↘.

ground   water
   land   trees

Z	T	I	K	Z	E	D
Q	S	R	A	R	E	N
D	D	R	E	L	R	U
E	N	T	H	E	V	O
L	A	F	R	N	S	R
W	L	O	Q	D	S	G

Horseshoe snake

AWESOME!

Snakes that live in deserts move by resting on their heads and tails and lifting the middle part of their bodies off the ground and swinging them forward in an S-shape. This movement, called sidewinding, helps keep their bellies off the scorching hot sand.

Snakes have a very good sense of smell that works in an unusual way. A snake's forked tongue flicks in and out constantly. This brings smells, such as the scent of animals to eat, or prey, into a special organ in the snake's mouth.

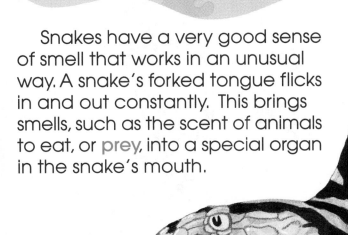

Viperine snake

Other organs in snakes' heads sense temperature. A snake moves its head from side to side to notice changes in the air temperature. The heat-sensing organ helps snakes find and strike warm-blooded prey in total darkness.

What's Long and Green?

One of the longest snakes is the common anaconda. It can grow as long as 30 feet! Look at the graph. About how many feet longer is the school bus than the anaconda? _____ How much longer is the anaconda than the alligator? _____

Length in feet

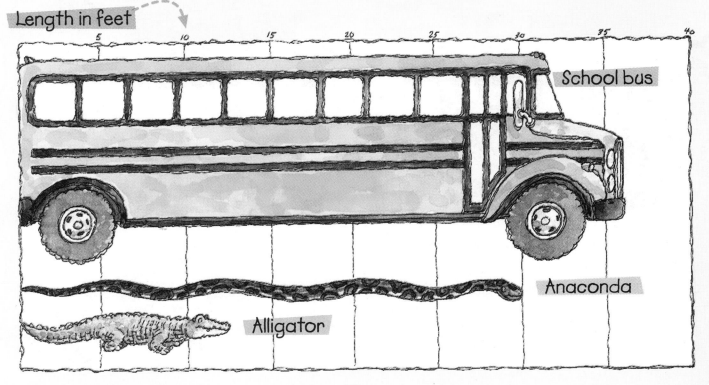

5   10   15   20   25   30   35   40

School bus

Anaconda

Alligator

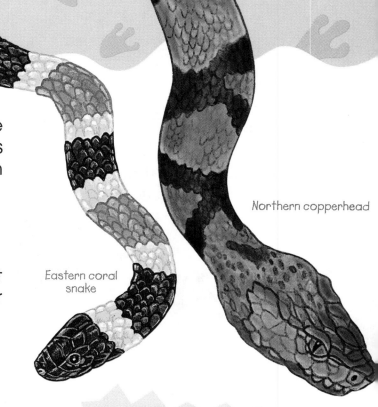

Snakes defend themselves in various ways. Their patterns and colors help some snakes blend with their surroundings. Others have bright colors and patterns that warn enemies to stay away.

Many snakes make warning sounds, such as hissing or rattling. A few kinds of snakes puff up, or **inflate**, parts of their body to scare enemies. Some snakes shoot poison, or **venom**, from their fangs into their prey to kill it.

Northern copperhead

Eastern coral snake

Timber rattler

Others wrap themselves around their prey and squeeze the breath out of it.

AWESOME!

Most snakes lay eggs, sometimes as many as 100 at a time. A few kinds of snakes give birth to live young. Most newly hatched or born snakes are on their own—their mothers don't stay around to take care of them.

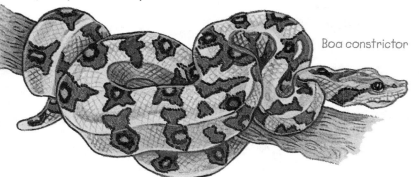

Boa constrictor

You mean snakes eat lizards like me?

Small snakes eat mice and rats, fish, birds, eggs, and small reptiles. Big ones eat large animals, such as goats or even alligators. Most snakes swallow their prey whole. Their jaws unhinge so their mouths can expand enough to fit the food through. Snakes can go for as long as a year between meals.

Snake Defenses

Match the defenses to the snakes.
Write the correct letters in the boxes.

A. warning sounds

B. warning colors

C. protective colors

D. changes in shape

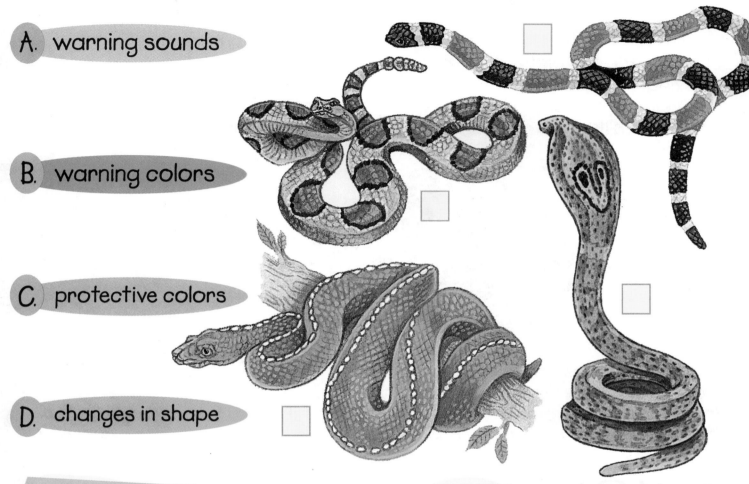

What's Wrong with the Sentences?

These sentences are false. Change or add a word in each one to make the sentence true.

1. The anaconda can grow as long as ten feet.

2. Most snakes take care of their babies.

3. Snakes that live in forests move by sidewinding.

4. Snakes use their fangs to sense smells.

TALK ABOUT TURTLES

Turtles are the only reptiles with shells. A turtle's shell is made of plates. The top plates, or scutes, are made of a material like your fingernails. The bottom plates are bony. The shell is part of the skeleton, so it can never be left behind. When in danger, a turtle pulls its head and legs into its shell for protection.

Spotted turtle

Some turtles live in water most of the time, but they breathe air. Most kinds of turtles eat plants and animals. Snapping turtles are fierce hunters with powerful jaws. They eat fish, frogs, salamanders, and even baby alligators.

Tortoises are turtles that live only on land. They eat plants. Gopher tortoises eat grasses and fruits.

All turtles and tortoises lay their eggs on land. Many female sea turtles bury their eggs on the same beach where they were hatched. When the eggs hatch, the babies run for the water. Most of the babies are eaten before they get to the ocean.

WRITE NOW!

Imagine that you carry your home around with you as a turtle does. What is your house like? Write a description.

Turtle Race!

How many baby turtles do you see? _____

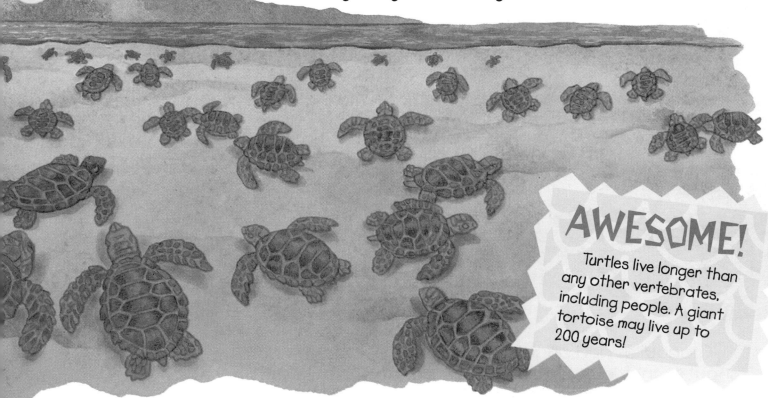

AWESOME!

Turtles live longer than any other vertebrates, including people. A giant tortoise may live up to 200 years!

You can tell whether a turtle lives mostly on land or in the water by the shape of its shell. Most land turtles, such as the side-necked turtle, have high domed shells. Water turtles, the painted turtle is one, have flatter shells.

Side-necked turtle   Painted turtle

Land or water?

Predict whether these turtles live in the water or on land by the shape of their shells. Write land or water on the line under each picture.

1._____   2._____   3._____   4._____

Talk About Turtles **47**

CLEVER CROCODILES (ALLIGATORS, TOO)

You've probably seen crocodiles and alligators at a zoo or in pictures. Could you tell the crocodiles from the alligators? Their snouts and teeth are clues. A crocodile's snout is narrower than an alligator's, and it has a pair of bottom teeth that show when its mouth is shut. Both crocodiles and alligators live near water in warm parts of the world.

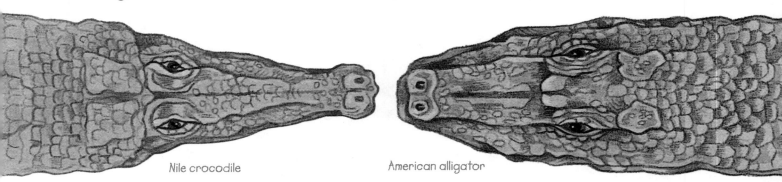

Nile crocodile

American alligator

Crocodiles and alligators have eyes, ears, and nostrils on top of their snout so they can hide themselves underwater as they hunt. Fast swimmers with strong jaws and big teeth, they eat just about any animal they can catch!

AWESOME!

Alligators in zoos have lived as long as 56 years. Crocodiles have lived up to 13-1/2 years. How much longer have alligators lived than crocodiles?

_____

_____

What a grin!

Like most reptiles, crocodiles and alligators lay eggs. The mother alligator guards the eggs until they hatch and protects the young alligators for a year or more. Some crocodiles guard their nests, too.

The Nile crocodile guards her eggs. After the eggs hatch, she carries her babies gently in her mouth from their nest on land to the river. The young crocodiles stay with her for several weeks before they swim off on their own.

AWESOME!

Crocodiles cool off by resting with open mouths. They don't need to floss their teeth. Crocodiles let birds remove the food that's stuck in their teeth.

Get to the River

Help the mother Nile crocodile get her babies safely from their nest to the river.

REPTILE ROUNDUP

AWESOME!

The tuatara (too-uh-tar-uh) looks like a lizard but is actually the last of a large group of reptiles that lived before the dinosaurs. Tuataras can be found only in parts of New Zealand.

Reptile Search & Sort

Circle the reptile names in the puzzle. Then write the names of the reptiles where they belong in the chart.

anaconda   python   gecko
iguana   tortoise   chameleon
alligator   boa

O	I	R	T	B	O	A	E	T	E
C	A	L	L	I	G	A	T	O	R
H	Z	N	R	S	U	D	H	R	B
A	D	G	A	R	A	E	B	T	R
M	R	E	Q	C	N	R	S	O	L
E	L	C	S	N	O	E	M	I	N
L	N	K	C	O	N	N	A	S	H
E	H	O	M	E	L	E	D	E	D
O	K	P	Y	T	H	O	N	A	N
N	A	T	I	G	U	A	N	A	B

Crocodiles & Alligators

Snakes

Turtles & Tortoises

Lizards

WHAT IS AN AMPHIBIAN?

Toads, frogs, salamanders, and some other animals are amphibians (am-**fib**-ee-uhnz). These animals are cold-blooded, have backbones, and as adults most kinds breathe through lungs just as reptiles do. But amphibians have lived on Earth much longer than reptiles. Amphibians have skin without scales. They live part of their lives in the water and part on land.

Scientists have divided amphibians into three groups. Frogs and toads have four legs and no tail, salamanders have long tails and two or four legs, and caecilians (suh-**sil**-ee-uhnz) have no legs and look like large earthworms.

Leopard frog

Cascades frog

Red salamander

Caecilian

I'm Nando. That's short for Fernando Frog.

Lots of animals snack on amphibians. Help Nando escape from his enemies.

Nando Needs Help!

What Is an Amphibian?   **51**

Alike and Different

Look at the circles with the words Amphibians and Reptiles. Write the letter for a way in which amphibians are different from reptiles under Amphibians. Write the letter for a way in which reptiles are different from amphibians under Reptiles. Where the circles overlap, write three letters for the qualities the animals share.

a. scaly skin

b. most breathe with lungs

c. skin without scales

d. vertebrates

e. cold-blooded

Amphibians

Reptiles

AWESOME!
Like lizards and snakes, amphibians shed their skin as they grow. They usually eat the old skin.

COOL WORD
The word amphibia means "double life." In what way do amphibians lead a double life?

Most young amphibians, or larvae (lar-vee), begin their lives in the water. They breathe through gills as fish do. Have you ever seen a tadpole? Tadpoles are the larvae of frogs.

Over time, two weeks to several months, the larvae grow and change into adults that look very different from the larvae. Most adults leave the water and live on land.

I started out as a tadpole, but now I hop around on land. Read about the parts of my life.

The Life of a Frog

Number the life stages of the frog in the right order.

Larvae have wide tails for swimming.

Adult frogs live in and out of the water.

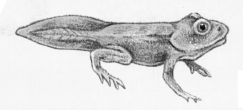

The tails of these larvae are shorter, and they breathe with lungs. Legs are growing and eyes are moving to the top of their heads. The larvae spend part of their time on land.

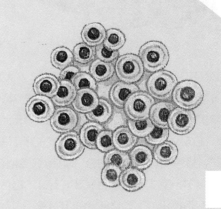

Eggs have gooey jelly around them instead of shells.

SHY SALAMANDERS

Italian cave salamander

Salamanders are shy animals that usually come out only at night. They look like lizards, except their skin is moist and smooth and their heads are rounder.

Olm

Crested newt

Salamanders that live in water all or most of their lives can breathe through their skin and with their gills and lungs. The mudpuppy's gills allow it to breathe oxygen dissolved in water.

AWESOME!

The name salamander comes from a word that means "fire animal." People once believed that salamanders were born from fire because they often came out of burning logs. Today we know that salamanders live in logs and crawl out when the logs burn.

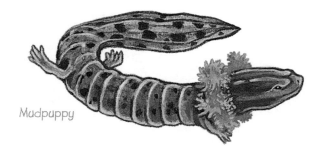

Mudpuppy

Spotted salamander

Salamanders that spend most or all of their lives on land may live under the ground, in rotting logs, under leaves, or even in trees. They must stay out of the sun to protect their moist, sensitive skin.

The adult spotted salamander spends most of its time hiding on the forest floor. At night, it hunts worms and insects. It grows to be about nine inches long.

Why do you think salamanders hunt for food at night?

_____

_____

_____

Salamander Code

Help! I just lost a leg. What should I do?
Use the code to answer the question.

a o n G w r t e h
▲ ✳ ❖ ■ ◎ ✴ ★ ◉ ✜

□ □ □ □ □ □ □ □ □ □ □ □ □ □ □ □!

■ ✴ ✳ ◎   ▲ ❖ ✳ ★ ✜ ◎ ✴   ✳ ❖ ◎

Would a Salamander Live Here?

Draw salamanders in the places they could live.

FANTASTIC FROGS

European green tree frog

There are almost 4,000 different kinds of frogs, and they live in every part of the world except the frozen Antarctic. Frogs have smooth, moist skin the same as salamanders do, but their bodies are very different. Frogs have long, strong back legs for jumping.

Ornated horned frog

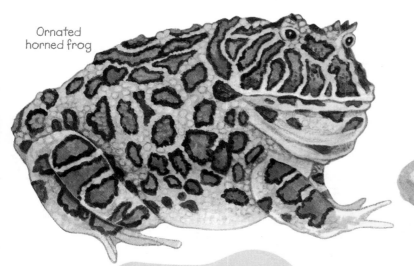

Common bullfrog

River frog

Froggy Math

1. The biggest frog is the Goliath frog of Africa. It is about one foot, or 12 inches, long. The smallest kinds are only about 1/2 inch long. How much longer is the biggest frog than the smallest?

_____

2. Many frogs can leap 20 times the length of their bodies. If a person four feet tall could do that, how far could the person jump?

_____

Gliding frog

3. The gliding frog uses its webbed feet to "fly" 50 feet through the air. How much longer is that than a 30-foot anaconda?

_____

Most frogs' eyes are large. They are set at the side of the head so the frogs can watch all around for danger. Some frogs' skins have bright colors to warn enemies to stay away.

Most frogs have colors and patterns that match their surroundings. This camouflage (kam-uh-flahzh) helps them hide from animals that want to eat them. Here's one example. The Asian leaf frog lives on forest floors. Its brown-and-yellow coloring and flat, pointy body make it look like a dead leaf.

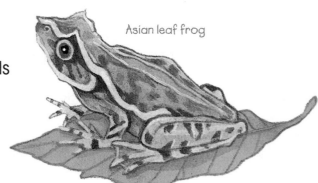

Asian leaf frog

Hide and Seek

How many frogs can you find in this picture? Circle them.

HOP ALONG TOADS

Toads look quite a bit like frogs, but they are different in some ways. Toads have dry, bumpy skin, not smooth, moist skin. They have plumper bodies and shorter back legs than frogs do. Because their legs are short, they can't leap like frogs. Instead, most toads hop.

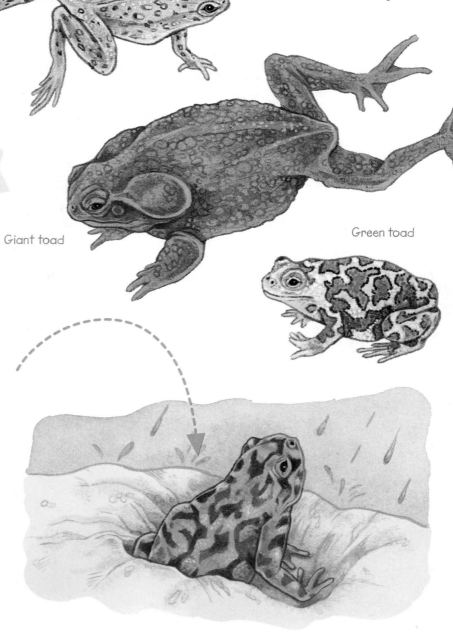

Midwife toad

Yosemite toad

Giant toad

Green toad

AWESOME!

Some people believe that if you touch a toad you'll get warts. You don't have to be a toad expert to know that isn't true!

Toads grow up in water, but most kinds spend much of their lives on land. Even land toads must keep their bodies from getting too dry. The spadefoot toad lives in hot, dry places. It keeps from drying out by burrowing underground. It may stay below the ground for months without eating. After a rainfall, it comes up at night and hunts for food.

Great Plains toad

Some male toads can puff up their throats to make noises that sound like flutes. Female toads can't do this.

Like frogs, many toads have long, sticky tongues that they use to catch worms, insects, and other small animals.

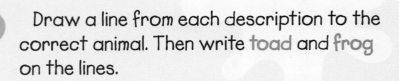

Toad or Frog?

Draw a line from each description to the correct animal. Then write toad and frog on the lines.

smooth and moist

short

plump

hop

dry and bumpy

long

leap

thin

_____

_____

AMPHIBIAN FUN

Name That Amphibian

Decide which kind of amphibian is talking. Write its name.

salamander   frog   toad

I think hopping is more dignified than leaping.

I'm shy. People used to think I came from fire.

I can jump higher than anybody!

1. _____

2. _____

3. _____

Fact or Fiction?

Write true or false after each sentence.

1. Frogs have smooth, moist skin. _____

2. Most salamanders come out at night. _____

3. Toads are better jumpers than frogs. _____

4. Some salamanders live in water. _____

5. Many frogs have bulging eyes to help them hide. _____

write now!

In one fairy tale, a princess kisses a frog and turns him into a prince. Make up your own amphibian fairy tale.

THE FUTURE OF REPTILES AND AMPHIBIANS

Although reptiles and amphibians have been around for millions of years, in many parts of the world they may not last much longer. Some reptiles and amphibians have already become extinct, or died off. These animals will never be seen again.

Here are some of the problems that threaten reptiles and amphibians.

- Air and water pollution caused by people is very harmful to these animals.

- Many reptiles and amphibians have lost their homes because people have built roads and houses where the animals live.

- Many reptiles and amphibians are taken from their wild homes to be sold. Animals such as snakes, turtles, and salamanders usually die when they are kept as pets.

Action Plan

Make a plan to help reptiles and amphibians.
Write three ideas or steps of your plan.

_____

_____

_____

AWESOME!

The International Union for Conservation of Nature is working to make conditions better for amphibians all over the world. Write them to learn how you can help.

IUCN Species Survival Commission,
c/o Chicago Zoological Society,
Brookfield, IL 60503

MORE ABOUT REPTILES AND AMPHIBIANS

Books

Reptiles and Amphibians
 by Catherine Herbert Howell
What Is a Reptile?
 by Robert Snedden
Salamanders by Cherie Winner
Scaly Babies: Reptiles Growing Up
 by Ginny Johnston and Judy Cutchins
Slippery Babies: Young Frogs, Toads, and Salamanders
 by Ginny Johnston and Judy Cutchins
Lizards by Claudia Schneiper
Amazing Crocodiles and Reptiles
 by Mary Ling
Amazing Snakes by Alexandra Parsons
Amazing Lizards by Trevor Smith

Internet Resources & CD-ROMs

Bill's Wildlife Links
 http://cccweb.com/wildlife.html
The World of Reptiles
 http://www.remedia.com
Froggy Page
 http://www.frog.simplenet.com

Video & Audio

Reptile
 eyewitness video produced by Dorling Kindersley
My Best Friend Is a Salamander
 audio cassette by Peter Himmelman, Baby Music Boom

ANSWERS

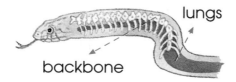

Page 34
Total # of reptiles: 12
The girl is not a reptile.

Page 37

Page 40

```
 ¹d i n o s a u r ³s
   ²i g         l
    u          ⁴f o u r
    a            g
 ⁵t o n g u e     s
  a      a
  i
  l
  s
```

Page 47
35

1. land
2. water
3. land
4. water

Page 48
42-1/2 years

Page 35

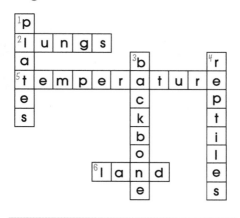

lungs

backbone

Page 38

```
¹p
²l u n g s
 a         ³b         ⁴r
⁵t e m p e r a t u r e
 e         c          p
 s         k          t
           b          i
           o          l
        ⁶l a n d       e
           e          s
```

Page 42

```
Z T I K Z E D
Q S R A R E N
D D R E L R U
E N T H E V O
L A F R N S R
W L O Q D S G
```

Page 36
Antarctica
Most children will guess
that Antarctica is too
cold for reptiles.

Page 39
Gila monster

Page 41
1. Komodo dragon
2. skink
3. gecko
4. iguana
5. flying dragon

Page 43
About 6 feet
About 18 feet

Page 45

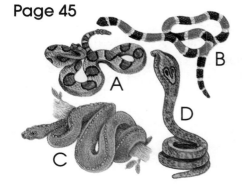

1. The anaconda can grow
   as long as 30 feet.
2. Most snakes don't take
   care of their babies.
3. Snakes that live in deserts
   move by sidewinding.
4. Snakes use their tongues
   to sense smells.

ANSWERS

Page 49

Page 50

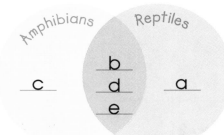

O	I	R	T	B	O	A	E	T	E
C	A	L	L	I	G	A	T	O	R
H	Z	N	R	S	U	D	H	R	B
A	D	G	A	R	A	E	B	T	R
M	R	E	Q	C	N	R	S	O	L
E	L	C	S	N	O	E	M	I	N
L	N	K	C	O	N	N	A	S	H
E	H	O	M	E	L	E	D	E	D
O	K	P	Y	T	H	O	N	A	N
N	A	T	I	G	U	A	N	A	B

Crocodiles & Alligators

alligator

Snakes

anaconda
boa
python

Turtles & Tortoises

tortoise

Lizards

gecko
chameleon
iguana

Page 51

Page 52

Amphibians   Reptiles

c

b
d
e

a

Page 53

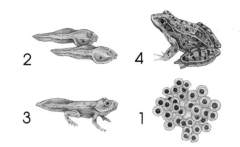

2   4

3   1

Page 54

Most children will write that salamanders hunt at night to avoid the sun.

Page 55

Grow another one!

Children should draw salamanders in each of the environments except the desert.

Page 57

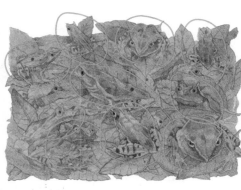

Page 56

1. 11-1/2 inches
2. 80 feet
3. 20 feet

Page 59

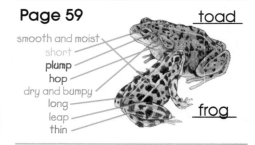

smooth and moist
short
plump
hop
dry and bumpy
long
leap
thin

toad

frog

Page 60

1. toad
2. salamander
3. frog

1. true
2. true
3. false
4. true
5. false